D0461319

Calvin Coolidge

Calvin Coolidge

R. Conrad Stein

AMERICA'S
30TH
PRESIDENT

Children's Press®
A Division of Scholastic Inc.
New York / Toronto / London / Auckland / Sydney
Mexico City / New Delhi / Hong Kong
Danbury, Connecticut

Library of Congress Cataloging-in-Publication Data

Stein, R. Conrad.
    Calvin Coolidge / by R. Conrad Stein.
        p. cm.—(Encyclopedia of presidents. Second series)
Includes bibliographical references and index.
  ISBN 0-516-22960-5
    1. Coolidge, Calvin, 1872–1933—Juvenile literature. 2. Presidents—United
States—Biography—Juvenile literature. [1. Coolidge, Calvin, 1872–1933.
2. Presidents.] I. Title. II. Series.
E792.S735 2004
973.91'5'092—dc22   2003027245

Contents

Chapter 1

The Education of a President

A Tame Leader for Wild Times ———

In the 1920s, a man in Minnesota claimed he set a world record by bobbing up and down in the water 1,843 times. An ex-sailor named "Shipwreck" Kelly made headlines by sitting on top of a flagpole for up to ten days. The 1920s was a decade of fads, folly, and ballyhoo. The ten-year span was called the Roaring Twenties because of its loud music and its young people who seemed to live only for their own pleasure. Years later, the writer F. Scott Fitzgerald looked back at the Roaring Twenties and said, "The restlessness approached hysteria. The parties were bigger. The pace was faster."

In stark contrast to these wild times stood the American president, Calvin Coolidge. For 5 years and 214 days—from August 3, 1923 to March 4, 1929—Calvin Coolidge held the most important office in the land. Many Americans regarded him as an anchor connecting the country to the old days when society seemed less complicated. Coolidge was popular. The 1920s was a time of general prosperity, and the public credited Coolidge with promoting the nation's wealth. In fact, the era was often called "Coolidge Prosperity." In addition, the president was honest. Not even his bitterest political enemies could accuse Coolidge of a crooked or an underhanded act.

Most of all he was "Silent Cal." He believed in wasting nothing, including words. If one politician made a speech that lasted an hour, Coolidge followed with a speech lasting five minutes. His close-mouthed style of leadership became a national joke. Calvin Coolidge, who had a dry but clever sense of humor, was not above adding to that joke himself. According to one story, a woman once said to him, "Mr. Coolidge, I made a bet with my friend that I could get more than three words out of you."

Coolidge answered, "You lose."

A Farm Youth

During the 1800s, most Americans still lived and worked on farms. The land they tilled had a way of shaping their personalities. Those who worked poor soil became frugal and *stoical*. They learned to endure disappointments, they thanked God for every success, and they wasted nothing. Rural Vermont was a beautiful land, but its soil was strewn with rocks and its winters were harsh. This rather stingy soil shaped Calvin Coolidge. Throughout his life he was thrifty, hard-working, and cautious.

John Calvin Coolidge was born in the farming village of Plymouth Notch, Vermont, on July 4, 1872. He was named John Calvin after his father, but to avoid confusion the family simply called him Calvin. He later dropped the first name John. He was the only American president to be born on the Fourth of July. A sturdy breed of men and women inhabited the villages of Vermont in Coolidge's youth. Most families made do with very little, and no one lived in splendor. Although it was hard to tell, the Coolidge family was one of the more prosperous in its small community. The Coolidges owned a farm and a country store. The family had deep roots in New England. Calvin Coolidge's great-great-grandfather arrived in 1780 from Great Britain.

New England Yankees

The region called New England is made up of six present-day states: Maine, New Hampshire, Vermont, Massachusetts, Rhode Island, and Connecticut. It was settled in the 1600s and 1700s mainly by immigrants from Britain. New Englanders established the first newspapers, libraries, primary schools, and colleges in the American colonies. Over the years, they came to be known as Yankees and became famous for "Yankee ingenuity," a special ability to make a living from the rocky New England soil.

☆ ☆ ☆

The birthplace of Calvin Coolidge in Plymouth Notch, Vermont.

Calvin's father, John Coolidge, was a prominent man in his community. The elder Coolidge held several public positions including justice of the peace and tax collector. He even managed the town dog pound. As Calvin was growing up, his father was elected to several terms in the Vermont Legislature. Calvin later wrote, "My father had qualities that were greater than any I possess. . . . He always stuck to the truth. It always seemed possible for him to form an unerring judgement of men and things."

The central figure in young Calvin's life was his mother. Victoria Coolidge suffered from ill health during Calvin's childhood. She loved literature and poetry and shared this love with Calvin and his sister Abigail, born three years after Calvin. Calvin grew up with the works of great writers such as William Shakespeare, Scottish novelist Walter Scott, and the poet Alfred, Lord Tennyson.

Victoria Coolidge, Calvin's mother, died when he was only twelve years old.

Calvin attended grade school in a one-room country schoolhouse. He was well be-haved, but he showed no particular brilliance. One of his earliest teachers recalled, "He was not an inquisitive boy. He seldom asked for an explanation of anything we had at hand." Perhaps Calvin failed to participate in classroom discussions because he was hampered by almost painful shyness. He once wrote to a friend, "When I was a little fellow . . . I would go into a panic if I heard strange voices in the house. I felt I just couldn't meet people and shake hands with them."

Calvin Coolidge was a good-looking boy with bright red hair and pale skin covered with freckles. One of his nicknames was Red. He cared little for sports, but

Calvin at about seven years old and his younger sister Abigail.

he did enjoy sledding with friends in the winter. He was uncomfortable in large groups and liked to ride his horse alone through the Vermont forests. Farmwork took up most of his time. Calvin mended fences, pitched hay, and milked cows. Perhaps farm chores helped him overcome the loneliness of his youth.

Tragedy struck the Coolidge family when Calvin was twelve years old. His mother died suddenly at age 39. Historians today believe she suffered from tuberculosis, a common disease that took many lives in that era. Her death left Calvin devastated. Almost a half century later he wrote of his mother's passing, "The greatest grief that can come to a boy came to me. Life was never to seem the same again."

Black River Academy

At age 13, Calvin enrolled in Black River Academy, a private high school in the nearby town of Ludlow. Attending the school was a long-standing tradition in the Coolidge family. Calvin's mother, father, and grandfather had studied there for several terms.

Ludlow was too far from Plymouth Notch for Calvin to travel there every day. This meant he had to leave home for the first time to live with a family nearer the school. On a winter day with snow covering the ground, John Coolidge drove his son to Ludlow in the family sleigh. In the back seat was a calf, which the father intended to ship to a market in Boston, Massachusetts, the largest city in New England. According to a famous story, when Calvin got off the sleigh in Ludlow, his father said, "Well, good-bye Cal. You may someday, if you work hard, get to Boston." The father then pointed to the calf in the rear of the buggy and said dryly, "But this calf's going to beat you there."

At Black River Academy Calvin studied Greek, Latin, French, ancient history, and algebra. He did poorly his first year, having particular difficulty with algebra. On the other hand, history courses delighted him. He later wrote that stories of the ancient world fired his imagination: "I marched with the Ten Thousand [soldiers] of Xenophon, I witnessed the conflict around beleaguered Troy which doomed that proud city to pillage and flames."

Calvin was overjoyed in his third year when his sister Abigail also became a student at the academy. He and Abigail had always been very close. She was outgoing and quick to make friends, a delightful contrast to Calvin's shyness. But tragedy once more visited the Coolidge family. Abigail, who always enjoyed robust health, suddenly developed pains in her stomach. Abigail Coolidge died within a week, probably from appendicitis. She was 15 years old. Her brother Calvin was at her bedside when she passed away.

The death of Abigail strengthened the bond between Calvin and his father. The two were now all that was left of the once strong and happy family. Father and son remained lovingly close for the rest of their lives. In the years to come, Calvin Coolidge rarely displayed open affection toward others, but even when he was president he was not afraid to kiss his father in public.

In September 1891, Calvin Coolidge entered Amherst College, in Amherst, Massachusetts, 90 miles (145 kilometers) south of Plymouth Notch. The future president was 19 years old. The journey to Amherst was his first venture outside of the state of Vermont. No one else in his immediate family

Amherst College

Amherst College was founded in 1821. When Calvin Coolidge registered, it had 336 students, all men. The college was well respected in academic circles. Several Amherst students who graduated near Coolidge's time rose to prominence. Melvil Dewey (class of 1874) invented the Dewey decimal system, which libraries use to classify books; Harlan Fiske Stone (1894) became a law school dean, and Coolidge later appointed him to the U.S. Supreme Court. Clarence Birdseye, who attended Amherst around 1910, became a millionaire by developing and marketing frozen foods.

The library of Amherst College in Amherst, Massachusetts, as it appeared when Coolidge was a student there.

☆ ☆ ☆

had ever attended college. His first year there was a repeat of his first year at Black River Academy. He was lonely, homesick, and withdrawn. "A drabber, more colorless boy I never knew than Calvin Coolidge when he came to Amherst," wrote one of his classmates. Coolidge also did poorly in his studies.

The same classmate said, "[Coolidge] attended class regularly, but he did not show any great interest."

Traditionally the young men of Amherst dated young women from the nearby colleges of Smith and Mount Holyoke. Coolidge had no dates. He could not dance. His shyness prevented him from approaching girls during the few parties he attended. Most of his nights were spent alone in a rented room reading by the light of an oil lamp.

College life improved in his third year when he fell under the spell of a professor named Charles Garman. Teaching natural sciences and philosophy, Garman, a graduate of Yale Divinity School, was deeply interested in how a Christian should act in everyday life. He urged his students to serve others without looking for personal gain. Garman's lectures had a magnetic quality that captured the young men's imagination. In his autobiography Coolidge wrote, "We looked upon Garman as a man who walked with God."

Coolidge received high grades for the essays he wrote. He even wrote a short story. Called "Margaret's Mist," it concerned a young lady who makes the shocking discovery that her lover is a bandit. Coolidge tried to imitate a popular style of romantic fiction: "'Waldo Martin,' said the emotionless Margaret, 'I need no explanation. I know now. How I have loved you! How I've trusted you! Robber! Murderer! Betrayer!'" The story was published in Amherst's literary magazine,

Calvin Coolidge as a senior at Amherst.

but it received little attention. Coolidge never again tried writing fiction.

During his senior year, Coolidge entered an essay contest sponsored by a patriotic organization, the Sons of the American Revolution, on "The Principles Fought for in the American Revolution." After graduation, he was surprised to learn that he had won first prize. The award included a gold medal valued at $150, a stunning sum for a college student in those days.

Coolidge also discovered he was a good public speaker. While uncomfortable in one-on-one conversations, he was remarkably at ease when addressing a group. Some class speaking assignments allowed other students to ridicule or heckle the speaker. Coolidge had the knack of dismissing a heckler by making a witty remark.

Shortly before he graduated, Coolidge participated in a humorous college event called the "Plug Hat Race." Contestants, snappily dressed, with a silk hat and a walking stick, were required to run the length of the college athletic field. The last seven finishers had to treat the other participants to dinner. Coolidge was one of the last seven. While serving dinner, he listened to the winners relentlessly teasing the losers. Coolidge told the winners, "Remember, boys, the Good Book says the first shall be last and the last shall be first." His witty comeback proved to be *prophetic*.

Chapter 2

Law and Politics

When Calvin Coolidge graduated from Amherst in 1895, he might have returned to Vermont to start his career. Like many young men of his times, however, he chose to move from his small farm village to a town where there were greater opportunities. Coolidge settled in Northampton, Massachusetts, a town of 15,000 people only 5 miles (8 km) from Amherst. Here Calvin Coolidge would learn to be a lawyer. The law appealed to Coolidge. He believed law was the foundation of American life. He once said, "The observance of the law is the greatest solvent of public ills."

In those days there were two ways to become a lawyer—attend law school or "read" for the law while working as a clerk in a law office. Law school was expensive, and Coolidge did not want his father to pay more bills for tuition and books. So he took a job reading for the law in Northampton in the law offices of John Hammond and Henry Field. Both were Amherst graduates who were happy to provide an opportunity to a fellow graduate.

Coolidge made friends with men and women in the Northampton community. His neighbors thought of him as a dignified if somewhat solitary young man. Above all, he was a good listener. He sat in barbershops and chatted with other men. Though Coolidge said little, he absorbed every word he heard. One of his friends was Jim Lucey, an Irish-born shoemaker. Coolidge often went to the shoe repair shop, took a seat on a bench, and listened to Lucey tell fascinating stories about his life in Ireland.

In 1897, when he was 25 years old, Coolidge received his license to practice law from the state of Massachusetts. He set up a small office in Northampton and waited for clients to knock on his door. Few clients came his way, but Coolidge was not discouraged. He later wrote, "I fully expected to become the kind of country lawyer I saw around me, spending my life in the profession."

He was also attracted to another field—politics. In his autobiography, he said he believed that holding a political office would help him be a better lawyer. Coolidge was already a member of the Republican party like his father and grandfather before him. Both Vermont and rural Massachusetts were heavily Republican regions. During the 1896 presidential campaign, Coolidge urged his

As a young lawyer, Coolidge spent many days at court in the Northampton Court House.

Northampton neighbors to vote for the Republican William McKinley over the Democratic candidate William Jennings Bryan.

In 1898 Coolidge ran for the office of councilman in the city of Northampton. His district was mostly Republican. Still, he won the election by appealing to Democratic voters. Using sound Yankee reasoning, Coolidge figured that each time he won the vote of a Democrat, he really had won two votes—one vote for himself and another vote that would have been cast for his opponent. He reached out to Democrats by never saying unkind words about his opponents. In conducting campaigns Coolidge was always a gentleman, and he was respected for this policy.

The office of city councilman was a part-time position and Coolidge received no payment for his service. Coolidge made his living mostly through his law practice. Also, his father sent him money every now and then to help cover expenses. Coolidge accepted his father's help, but never said a word to others about the money. He was silently ashamed that although he was a lawyer and a minor officeholder, he still did not earn enough to pay his house rent. His finances improved in 1900, when he was appointed *city solicitor*. This part-time position, representing the town in local disputes, paid $600 a year.

The Lawyer Meets a Lady

Calvin Coolidge was deliberate in all matters, even love. There were rumors that he fell for a red-haired Northampton girl and was devastated when she refused to marry him. Those rumors have never been confirmed. More than likely, he hoped he would not fall in love and get married until he could afford to support a family.

Calvin Coolidge and his father, who provided support to his son from boyhood and lived to see him elected president.

Grace Anna Goodhue came from a fine family and, like Coolidge, was born in Vermont. That is where the similarities ended. She was talkative and outgoing, and she laughed easily. Her father was a long-standing member of the Democratic party. Grace studied at the University of Vermont. After graduation she got a job teaching deaf children at the Clarke School for the Deaf in Northampton.

One day Grace was watering flowers at the school when she looked up. Through a window she saw a thin young man, apparently in his long underwear, who was shaving while wearing a hat on his head. She tried not to stare, but thought it odd that anyone should shave with a hat on. Calvin Coolidge, the man who was shaving, returned her gaze through the window. Immediately Calvin fell in love and decided he would marry this lady. He still was not earning enough to properly support a family, but love waits for no man, not even a deliberate man like Calvin Coolidge.

Calvin and Grace were introduced by the owner of the rooming house where Calvin lived. They took long walks, went on picnics, and attended church socials and card parties. Calvin loved the long walks and disliked the social events. In those days before the automobile, Calvin and Grace rode the streetcar or walked when they went out.

Calvin Coolidge took his first ride in an automobile in 1904 when he was 32 years old. At the time cars were unreliable and expensive. They appealed to mechanics and to rich hobbyists. Coolidge thanked the man who gave him his first ride, but he said of the automobile, "It won't amount to much."

☆ ☆ ☆

In the summer of 1905, Calvin Coolidge unexpectedly showed up at the Goodhue home in Burlington, Vermont. Grace later described the conversation between her father and the future president:

"Up here on some law business, Mister Coolidge?" asked Grace's father.

"No," said Coolidge. "Up here to ask your permission to marry Grace."

A somewhat surprised Andrew Goodhue asked, "Does she know it?"

"No," came the answer, "but she soon will."

Calvin and Grace were married on October 4, 1905. She was 26 and he was 33 years old. During their small wedding party he was true to his image of Silent Cal. One woman arrived late and saw a well-dressed young man standing in a corner saying nothing. The woman knew that Grace was a teacher of the deaf, who often could not speak. She asked, "That young man standing by himself in the corner, is he one of Grace's pupils?"

Grace Goodhue in 1904. The next year she and Calvin Coolidge were married.

★ THE YOUNG MR. COOLIDGE ★

Climbing the Political Ladder ——————

The newlyweds rented a furnished house in Northampton. Following the customs of the time, Grace Coolidge stayed home and attended to all the domestic chores while Coolidge continued his law practice. Grace accepted her role, but was shocked when Calvin presented her with 52 pairs of socks with holes in them to be mended. He had apparently never mended a sock in his bachelor life. Grace asked him if he got married simply to find someone willing to repair his stockings. "No," said Calvin, "but I find it mighty handy."

In the spring of 1906 Grace Coolidge was pregnant. To prepare for the child, the couple rented a comfortable duplex with seven rooms. Rent was $28 a month. They had to watch their pennies as Calvin still earned very little. Even after Calvin was married, his father sent money to help the couple along. John Coolidge, the couple's first son, was born September 7, 1906. Calvin knew he must now work harder to support a growing family.

As a lawyer Coolidge served rich and poor clients, giving equal attention to both. One of his biographers wrote, "He was the kind of attorney who would go out late at night to draw up a dying Irish lady's will and charge her only five dollars instead of the usual twelve or fifteen." Coolidge became known in Northampton as an honest, efficient, and kind attorney. This reputation helped him climb the political ladder.

In 1906 Coolidge ran for the Massachusetts General Court, as the state legislature was known. Like the federal legislature, it was composed of a House of Representatives and a Senate. Coolidge sought a seat in the House of Representatives. He campaigned the old-fashioned way, by knocking on doors and speaking directly to the voters. He won by the slim margin of 264 votes over his Democratic opponent.

The General Court met in Boston, the state capital. Coolidge rented a room there at an inexpensive hotel called the Adams House. Wearing dark-colored business suits and saying little, he made no great first impressions on the state's political elite. A leading Democrat once looked at Coolidge and said, "This fellow is either a schoolteacher or an undertaker [funeral director] from the country. I don't know which."

Coolidge usually voted with other Republicans in the House, but he did not always answer his party's call. *Women's suffrage*, the movement to gain voting rights for women, was a burning issue at the time. Many Republicans opposed women's suffrage, but Coolidge supported the measure. He also approved of laws that required employers to pay women a minimum wage for their work.

Coolidge won a second term to the House of Representatives in November, 1907. Five months later his family was blessed with the birth of a second son. Calvin Coolidge Jr. was born April 13, 1908. Coolidge did not stand for reelection

As a state legislator, Coolidge lived part-time in Boston, the capital of Massachusetts. The city boasted historic buildings like the Old State House (bottom left) and new skyscrapers like the Ames Building (upper right).

that November, preferring to stay at home with his young family. The following year, however, local Republicans asked him to run for mayor of Northampton. He was elected in November 1909 and served for two one-year terms.

The Lawrence Strike

In 1911 Coolidge ran for a seat in the state senate and was elected. This was a major step up the political ladder, but now he was confronted a difficult challenge. Soon after he took office in early 1912, the American Woolen Company in Lawrence, Massachusetts, cut the wages of its 13,000 mill workers. The workers, who were already underpaid, went on strike. Into this dispute stepped a radical labor organization called the Industrial Workers of the World (the IWW). The city of Lawrence called in the state militia to protect the mills and keep peace. Many Massachusetts residents feared a labor war would break out in Lawrence and spread throughout the state. The General Court asked Senator Coolidge to head a committee to help settle the matter peacefully.

During a month of tense negotiations, Coolidge and his committee helped persuade the company to cancel its pay cut and to grant the workers a wage increase. The company also agreed to let the strikers return to work without penalty. The men and women returned to their jobs. Coolidge was hailed for his level-headed leadership in a time of crisis.

Strikers from textile mills in Lawrence march toward the mills in 1912. As a state senator, Coolidge helped settle the strike.

The Wobblies

The Industrial Workers of the World (IWW) was formed in 1905 and was the most *radical* labor organization in the country. The IWW hoped to organize all U.S. workers into a single large union to gain greater bargaining power with employers. IWW members were called "Wobblies." They were accused of encouraging workers to use violence during strikes. In the years after the Lawrence strike, the IWW lost its appeal to workers. Today the Wobblies are remembered for radical views and their spirited songs, which striking workers sang at IWW rallies. One of the most famous was "Solidarity Forever," which was sung to the tune of "The Battle Hymn of the Republic":

> When the union's inspiration through the workers' blood shall run,
> There can be no power greater anywhere beneath the sun.
> Yet what force on earth is weaker than the feeble strength of one?
>> But the union makes us strong!
>
> *Chorus:*
> Solidarity forever, Solidarity forever,
> Solidarity forever,
>> For the union makes us strong!

☆ ☆ ☆

Statewide Office

Coolidge was elected to four one-year terms in the Massachusetts State Senate. His family continued to live in Northampton. When the Senate was in session, Coolidge traveled to Boston and lived in a hotel there. As soon as the session was over, he returned home.

While serving in the Senate, Coolidge met a remarkable man named Frank Stearns. He was the first observer to see potential greatness in this otherwise ordinary politician. Stearns even dared to think that Calvin Coolidge might be president of the United States someday. The wealthy owner of a Boston department store, Stearns was almost 20 years older than Coolidge. Most important, Stearns was another Amherst graduate (class of 1878). In those days old school ties were strong bonds. A man was expected to boost the career of another man who had attended the same college.

Encouraged by Stearns, Coolidge announced in 1915 that he would run for lieutenant governor. The Republican candidate for governor was an experienced politician named Samuel McCall. The two men had vastly different styles. McCall made fiery speeches, while Coolidge addressed crowds in a calm and rational manner. The journalist William Allen White noted, "McCall could fill any hall in Massachusetts and Coolidge could empty it."

Yet with the help of Stearns, Coolidge gained wide support in his run for the second-highest office in the state. Both he and McCall were elected in November. Coolidge was sworn in as lieutenant governor on January 6, 1916. He had already climbed high on the political ladder. None of his friends—except perhaps Frank Stearns—dreamed that he would continue his climb all the way to the White House.

Chapter 3

Eyes on the Governor's Job ————

Calvin Coolidge served three one-year terms as lieutenant governor, from 1916 through 1918. While he occupied that office, his father sent him a $20 check. It was the last financial contribution made from father to son. Coolidge's modest income and style of life are a tribute to his integrity. Unlike many political leaders of his time, Coolidge refused to take advantage of his office to participate in private business deals that might have made him rich. He believed law and government service were noble professions which a person should pursue for noble reasons.

War and strife plagued the nation during Coolidge's time as lieutenant governor. In 1914, war had broken out in Europe between the Central Powers (Germany, Austria-Hungary, and others) and the Allied Powers (Great Britain, France, Russia, and others). In 1917 the

United States joined the war (now known as World War I) on the side of the Allies. Some two million American soldiers crossed the Atlantic to fight in the mud and trenches of France and Belgium. That same year, revolutions in Russia overturned the government of the czar and brought it under the control of militant Communists. Russia withdrew from the war, and its revolutions stirred fear of radical political groups in Europe and the United States.

On June 23, 1918, Coolidge announced that he would run for governor of Massachusetts. U.S. troops were embroiled in major battles that summer, and the country was gripped by extreme patriotism and hatred for the enemy. During the campaign, Coolidge jumped on the patriotic bandwagon. In one of his most emotional speeches, he said, "The past four years [have] shown the world the existence of a conspiracy against mankind of a vastness and a wickedness that could only be believed when seen in operation and confessed by its participants. This conspiracy was promoted by the German military despotism."

In November, the election was close. Coolidge defeated his Democratic opponent Richard Long by only 17,000 votes. Only days later, an *armistice* (an end to fighting while a peace treaty is negotiated) ended the war in Europe. On January 1, 1919, Calvin Coolidge was inaugurated governor of Massachusetts. Coolidge saw the end of the war as an opportunity for progress in Massachusetts.

Coolidge as governor of Massachusetts.

In his inaugural address, he turned to members of the state legislature and said, "It is your duty not only to reflect public opinion, but to lead it. Whether we are able to enter a new era in Massachusetts depends on you."

In fact, the end of the war unleashed conflict and violence in the United States. Workers, whose wages had been frozen during the war, wanted large increases. Violent labor strikes exploded around the country. In Seattle, Washington, workers staged a five-day general strike that shut down the entire city. Many Americans believed the Seattle workers were inspired by Communists, who hoped to encourage other strikes across the country. Government officials began investigating and arresting labor leaders and leaders of political parties considered to be socialist or communist.

In the meantime, Coolidge concentrated on more positive actions. He pushed for laws to ease the plight of poor people in Massachusetts. He signed an act raising pay for teachers saying, "We compensate liberally the manufacturer and the merchant, but we fail to appreciate those who guard the minds of our youth." He also backed a measure to give state bonuses of $100 to every returning war veteran. He said of veterans, "The nation that forgets its defenders will soon be forgotten."

Recalling his experience as a negotiator during the Lawrence strike, Coolidge also pressed the legislature to pass laws to reduce the workweek for women workers from 54 hours to 48 hours a week. Owners of the textile mills objected, but Coolidge dismissed their complaints. "We must humanize industry," he said, "or the system will break down."

Some of the governor's acts disturbed Frank Stearns, the wealthy store owner and Amherst graduate. Stearns was a conservative Republican who favored tax cuts, low government spending, and rights for big business. Coolidge tended to be conservative, but not to the extent Stearns wanted him to be. Still, Stearns knew that not even he could tell Calvin Coolidge what to do. One day a man seeking a high state job asked Stearns to put in a good word with the governor. The job-seeker reminded Stearns that he had great influence over Coolidge. Stearns replied, "Yes, perhaps more than you think, but it will last just as long as I don't try to use it, and not one minute longer."

The Boston Police Strike

In the steaming summer of 1919, Governor and Mrs. Coolidge took a brief vacation to Vermont. The heat and humidity of a Boston summer always bothered Calvin Coolidge. He felt it would be refreshing to get away to the Vermont farm country again. The governor soon had to rush back to Boston and confront the most dangerous situation in his political career.

Boston policemen were woefully underpaid. They worked long hours and fought dangerous criminals, yet they earned less money than the average factory hand. If they had been machinists or truck drivers they could join a union and go on strike to demand better pay and working conditions.

In August 1919, the frustrated police officers of Boston decided to form a union. Just the idea of unionized policemen worried safety-minded Bostonians. If police went on strike, who would protect them? Hoping to discourage the new union, Police Commissioner Edwin Curtis fired 19 union organizers. The union members were enraged, and on September 8, they voted by the overwhelming vote of 1,134 to 2 to go out on strike the next day.

At first governor Coolidge tried to stay out of the tense standoff in Boston, urging the city government to deal with the situation. Still, he knew the eyes of the nation were on Boston. The Seattle general strike lingered in everyone's memories. Many wondered if the Communists were behind the Boston police strike. Would such police strikes take place in other cities?

Trouble began on September 9, the first night of the strike. Huge crowds gathered in the center of the city, and soon gangs were breaking store windows and carting away the merchandise. In one neighborhood young men stole a barrel of whiskey and distributed drinks. Others broke into restaurants and helped themselves to free food. Without a police force, people felt helpless. It seemed that war might break out in Boston. The governor had to act.

Coolidge believed the police had a legitimate complaint. One Coolidge spokesman said, "Can you blame the police for feeling as they do when they get paid less than a streetcar conductor?" However, Coolidge insisted policemen had special responsibilities. They were not factory workers or carpenters. Their job was to protect the public, and going on strike was unthinkable.

Order was soon restored in Boston. Governor Coolidge called out 4,800 National Guard troops to patrol the city. In the next few days, the police union called off the strike and asked Commissioner Curtis to reinstate the striking officers while a settlement was being worked out. With Coolidge's approval, Curtis refused. He announced that all police officers who had gone out on strike had been dismissed, and he began hiring and training new police officers to replace them.

Samuel Gompers, the leader of the country's largest union, the American Federation of Labor, complained to Coolidge about the harsh treatment of the striking police officers. Coolidge replied in a public telegram: "There is no right to strike against the public safety by anybody, anywhere, any time." Those 15 words were electric. Newspapers across America printed them on page one. The *New York Herald* wrote, "It is fortunate that Massachusetts has a governor who . . . has

Above, Governor Coolidge inspects the Massachusetts National Guard during the Boston police strike in 1919.
At right, guardsmen protect a looted store.

the determination and patriotism to stand firm for the sovereignty and dignity of the Commonwealth [of Massachusetts]." For the first time, millions of Americans outside of Massachusetts became aware of the state's plainspoken governor.

In the wake of the police strike, the city of Boston agreed to provide its police force with large salary increases and improved working conditions. Two months later, Coolidge was easily reelected governor of Massachusetts.

Washington Calls

As 1920 began, Woodrow Wilson, a Democrat, had been president of the United States for seven years. He had led the country through a period of reform at home and of war overseas. He also helped establish the League of Nations, the first international organization to help end conflicts between nations. When Wilson returned from the peace conference in 1919, however, he faced growing opposition at home. The U.S. Senate refused to *ratify* (officially approve) the World War I peace treaty and refused to approve United States membership in the League of Nations. In October 1919, Wilson suffered a severe *stroke* (a stoppage of blood circulation in the brain). During his remaining months in office, he recovered very slowly from his illness, and his party struggled to find a new leader.

Looking ahead to the fall elections, the Republican party smelled victory. The American people were exhausted by reforms and war regulations during

Wilson's presidency. They were uncomfortable with the influx of immigrants and the struggles between labor and management. They were mourning the loss of more than 50,000 young Americans in World War I, and had begun to doubt that the war was worthwhile for the United States. People longed for the good old days before the war when things seemed simpler.

The Republican National Convention met in Chicago in the summer of 1920 to nominate its candidates for president and vice president. There was no single strong leader in the party, but there were many able Republican candidates. The Massachusetts delegation nominated Calvin Coolidge for president as its *favorite son*, or home-state hero. Most party members were hoping for a "safe" candidate, one who could win the presidency simply by making few or no mistakes on the campaign trail. The convention finally settled on Warren Harding, a senator from Ohio.

Calvin Coolidge was not at the Chicago convention, but many friends and supporters were there, led by Frank Stearns. Stearns was hoping the party would nominate Coolidge for president. When Harding was selected, Stearns set his goal on the vice presidency. To accomplish this, he distributed hundreds of copies of a book called *Have Faith in Massachusetts*, a collection of speeches by Calvin Coolidge. The speeches were clear and inspirational. Many delegates, even those who knew very little about Calvin Coolidge, became convinced he would be a

The Smoke-Filled Room

When voting began for the presidential nomination, a few leading candidates surged to the lead, but none of them had nearly enough votes to win the nomination. The delegates voted in ballot after ballot, but the totals remained about the same. Finally the convention adjourned, planning further balloting the next day.

Delegates gathered everywhere to discuss the candidates. It was clear that a compromise candidate was needed, but how would the choice be made? That night a group of the party's most powerful men gathered in Chicago's Blackstone Hotel to discuss the nomination. Meeting behind closed doors, they went through the candidates one at a time. Soon the room was filled with the smoke of their cigars. Finally, in the early morning hours, the leaders agreed to support Governor Harding for the nomination. The next morning, the word went out to delegates from many states. When the voting began, Harding's total rose higher on each ballot until he received the needed majority and the nomination.

In newspapers the next day, reporters described the bosses' meeting in the "smoke-filled room." They suggested that the nomination was won not by the delegates' votes but by the bosses' decision behind closed doors. Ever since, a "smoke-filled room" has suggested a meeting where decisions are made by a party's insiders, not by its regular members.

☆ ★ ☆

good running mate for Warren Harding. When balloting began for the vice presidential nomination, the convention seemed ready to support Coolidge above all others. He won the nomination with ease.

Coolidge and his wife were in a room at the Adams House hotel in Boston when they learned of his nomination. Coolidge received the news by telephone. He turned to his wife and said, "Nominated for vice president."

"You aren't going to take it, are you?" Grace Coolidge asked.

"Well—I suppose I'll have to," he replied.

Coolidge's reaction was true to his character. Throughout his career Coolidge rarely sought higher political offices openly. He preferred for nominations to come to him and to accept them with a modest shrug of his shoulders. When he met the press, he said, "The nomination for the vice presidency, coming to me unsought and unexpectedly, I accept as an honor and duty."

No Frequent Flyer

Before he was nominated for vice president, Coolidge traveled very little. He had never been west of the Appalachian Mountains. He had visited Washington, D.C., only once. Apparently he felt uneasy while he was away from home. Even after his presidency Coolidge shunned travel. He was the last American president who never in his life flew in an airplane.

☆ ★ ☆

Republican presidential candidate Warren Harding with vice-presidential candidate Coolidge in 1920.

After the convention Coolidge traveled to Washington to meet Harding for the first time. The two men enjoyed a breakfast of waffles and chipped beef. They discussed their campaign plans and especially their opponents. The Democrats had nominated Ohio governor James Cox for president and Assistant Secretary of the Navy Franklin D. Roosevelt for vice president. (Roosevelt would later become the 32nd president.)

Following an old Republican tradition, Harding waged a "front porch" campaign. Instead of traveling to speak to voters, he invited them to come to his hometown of Marion, Ohio, to visit him. Thousands of supporters traveled to Marion to shake his hand and hear him speak. Harding enjoyed the campaign, once observing that shaking hands "is the most pleasant thing I do." Harding also befriended newspaper reporters, some of whom lived in Marion through the summer. Coolidge took to the campaign trail and made speeches in Minnesota, Kentucky, and Tennessee. He did not enjoy traveling and it showed. His campaign speeches lacked fire and spirit.

Harding and Coolidge were supported by a huge Republican advertising campaign. Their pictures appeared in every town and village. The slogan for the

Women's Suffrage

The 19th Amendment to the Constitution, which allowed women to vote in federal elections, took effect in August of 1920, just in time for the presidential election. The long struggle to achieve women's suffrage had begun in 1848 at a small meeting of women's advocates in Seneca Falls, New York. Many feminist leaders, including Elizabeth Cady Stanton, Lucretia Mott, and Susan B. Anthony, devoted their lives to achieving voting privileges for women.

☆☆☆

The Coolidge family during the 1920 campaign. At upper left are Coolidge's son, Calvin Jr., his father John Calvin, and son John.

campaign came from one of Harding's speeches: "Back to Normalcy." The campaign leaders made a special point to appeal to women voters, who would be voting in a presidential election for the first time.

The low-key candidates and the attractive message struck a chord with voters. Harding and Coolidge won a huge landslide victory, defeating their Democratic opponents by the largest margin in history. They received 16 million votes to 9 million for Cox and Roosevelt. Calvin Coolidge was headed for Washington.

UNDER
The 19th
Amendment
I CAST MY
FIRST VOTE
Nov. 2nd, 1920

Harding
Coolidge

The Straight
Republican
Ticket

Lancaster, Pa.

A ribbon worn by Republican women during the 1920 campaign. This was the first presidential election in which they had the right to vote.

Chapter 4

A Look at the Roaring Twenties ————

On March 4, 1921, President Warren Harding and Vice President Calvin Coolidge took their oaths of office. The presidential inauguration marked the beginning of an era. A new government was sweeping into Washington, and the Roaring Twenties were just under way. No one then knew how revolutionary this new decade would prove.

Machines and household products transformed American life during the roaring years. In 1920 only one-third of American homes had electricity; by 1929 that figure had jumped to two-thirds. At the beginning of the decade, radio or "wireless" was used and understood by a small group of engineers and hobbyists. By 1925 more than 5 million American households had radios in their living rooms. The number of automobiles tripled in the 1920s. Americans became so car-crazy they sacrificed other needs in order to buy a "gas buggy." A reporter asked a farm woman why she bought a car even though her family did not have a bathtub. The woman replied, "Because you can't drive to town in a bathtub."

One of the dominant issues of the decade was Prohibition. In 1920 the 18th Amendment to the Constitution became law. It prohibited the manufacture, sale, or transportation of "intoxicating liquors"—any beverages that contained alcohol. Millions, including a majority of Republicans, had supported the law, but it quickly proved almost impossible to enforce. No law in American history was so universally violated.

Illegal taverns, called speakeasies, soon sprang up. By the mid-1920s an estimated 32,000 "speaks" operated in New York City alone. A secret knock on a door followed by whispered words such as, "Harry sent me," allowed a person to enter one of the forbidden saloons. Gangsters took over the distribution and sale of alcohol and became rich and powerful. The most notorious was Chicago's Al Capone. *Bootleggers*, those who made illegal liquor, became folk heroes because they violated the unpopular law and made illegal alcohol available.

The young people of the Twenties gained a scandalous reputation. Gaining new freedom to be independent, traveling in cars, going to the movies, and listening to the popular "swing" music, they outraged their parents and older Americans by their rebellious behavior. Young ladies wore dresses with hems cut shockingly

Federal agents destroy an illegal saloon during Prohibition, when the law prohibited the sale of alcoholic drinks.

short, barely covering their knees. New music with a heavy rhythmic beat and fast dances such as the Charleston appealed to the young and alarmed their parents.

President Harding —————————————————————

Into this new environment stepped President Warren Harding. A successful newspaper publisher, he was handsome and charming, but he seemed unprepared for the responsibilities of his new job. Before his nomination, he told one reporter that his position in the U.S. Senate was "far more to my liking than the presidency possibly could be."

Harding allowed Congress to determine the country's domestic policy. He claimed that setting policy was a congressional responsibility. Leaving the task to them also relieved him of making difficult decisions. The president was painstakingly slow when it came to making up his mind. He once told a secretary, "I can't make a thing out of this tax problem. . . . I listen to one side and they seem right, and then . . . I talk to the other side and they seem just as right, and here I am where I started."

Above all, Harding wanted to be loved by the American people. During his first year in office he accomplished this mission. News photos showed him always jovial and smiling. His image was that of a jolly grandfather. This friendly portrait hid a variety of shady deals and corrupt practices that later came to light.

Although he appointed a few able men to his cabinet, Harding preferred to spend his time with a group of friends and advisers that became known as the "Ohio gang." Not all were from Ohio and not all held high government positions. Some simply enjoyed the all-night poker games the president liked to attend. Among the Ohio gang, Attorney General Harry Daugherty stood out. He had been a friend and supporter of Harding since both were young men in Ohio politics. Daugherty was a shrewd political operator, but he seemed to have few qualifications to serve as the chief law enforcement officer of the United States.

Vice President Coolidge

Calvin Coolidge was not a member of President Harding's Ohio gang. In fact, he and the president were exact opposites. Where Harding was loud and boisterous, Coolidge was quiet and reserved. Where Harding enjoyed late-night parties and card games, Coolidge went to bed early. In addition, Harding's wife Florence did not care for Calvin Coolidge, seeming to consider him to be little more than a country bumpkin.

The main duty of a vice president is to be ready to lead the nation if the president dies. This was largely a matter of waiting, and Coolidge found himself with little to do. He served as president of the Senate. According to the Constitution, however, he could only cast a vote if the Senate was tied. Such a tie

As vice president, Coolidge befriended the Senate pages, young men who served as messengers on the Senate floor. Here they cheer him on the steps of the Capitol.

never occurred during his term. Since he was rarely consulted by the president or given other duties, Coolidge found the vice presidency perhaps the easiest government job he ever held.

Although he was the number two leader in the land, Coolidge remained largely out of the public eye. He enjoyed telling a story that illustrated his low profile in Washington. The Coolidges lived at the Willard Hotel, near the White House. One day a small fire broke out there, and all guests were ordered to leave the building. The blaze was soon put out. When Coolidge and his wife tried to return to their rooms, they were stopped by a fire marshal.

"Who are you?" demanded the fire marshal.

Coolidge replied, "I'm the vice president."

"What are you vice president of?" the marshal asked.

"I am vice president of the United States," Coolidge said.

The fireman nodded and said, "Come right on in. I thought you were the vice president of the hotel."

That Fateful Day

In July 1923, the Coolidge family visited Calvin's father in Plymouth Notch, Vermont. The vice president and his sons, John and Calvin, pitched in and did chores on the family farm. Meanwhile, President Harding had taken a long speaking tour of the western United States and Alaska. Late in July, he was on his way home when he fell ill. Newspapers reported that he had eaten spoiled seafood. During a stay in a San Francisco hotel, his condition seemed to improve. Then on the night of August 2, the president died suddenly. Historians believe the president died not from food poisoning, but from advanced heart disease.

Coolidge and the people of Plymouth Notch were among the last Americans to hear the shocking news. The Coolidge house had no electricity and no telephone. The nearest phone was in a store across the road. An operator tried desperately to reach the store, but it was 10:30 at night, and Miss Florence Cilley, who lived in back of the store, was fast asleep and did not hear the phone ring. The vice president's secretary was staying at a hotel in the nearby town of Bridgewater. When he couldn't reach Coolidge, he and other staff members piled into a car and raced over the bumpy roads to the Coolidge farm.

Finally the town was aroused. Calvin Coolidge walked across the road to the store and made a long-distance phone call to Charles Evans Hughes, the secretary of state. Hughes urged him to be sworn in as president immediately. They agreed that Coolidge's father, who was a notary public, was qualified to administer the oath of office. Coolidge returned to the house and dictated a note of sympathy to Mrs. Harding, who had been at her husband's bedside. Then at 2:45 on the morning of August 3, 1923, John Coolidge administered the oath of office to his son Calvin, reading the words of the oath by the light of a kerosene lamp.

Coolidge (left) is sworn in as president in Plymouth Notch by his own father on August 3, 1923.

"I Will Execute the Office of President"

The Constitution says a president must take an oath of office before assuming duties. It does not say who should administer that oath. The oath is usually given by the Chief Justice of the United States, but in an emergency any public official can perform the function. The Coolidge oath of office marked the first and only time a president was sworn in by his father. Coolidge later took the oath again before a District of Columbia judge. The exact words a new president must say are spelled out in the Constitution: "I do solemnly swear (or affirm) that I will faithfully execute the Office of President of the United States, and will to the best of my ability, preserve, protect, and defend the Constitution of the United States."

★ ★ ★

Years later Coolidge was asked about his feelings on suddenly becoming president. With characteristic brevity, he answered, "I thought I could swing it."

Later that morning President Calvin Coolidge packed up to return to Washington. The car had gone less than a mile when Coolidge asked the driver to stop in front of a small rural cemetery. Coolidge walked among the gravestones and stopped in front of his mother's grave. Although she had died when Calvin was only twelve, her loving memory always remained in his thoughts. He later wrote, "It had been a comfort to me during my boyhood when I was troubled to be near her last resting place, even in the dead of night. Some way, that morning, she seemed very near to me."

Completing Harding's Term

As Coolidge took office, the scandals of the Harding years were just being exposed to the public. Evidence from the investigations of Harding's appointees began to appear on the front pages of newspapers across the country. The most serious of the scandals became known as Teapot Dome. Secretary of the Interior Albert Fall (who resigned from Harding's cabinet early in 1923), had gained control of the oil reserves of the U.S. Navy. Without the knowledge of President Harding or Congress, he negotiated leases with private oil companies that allowed them to pump out oil for private sale. One of the largest reserves was in Teapot Dome, Wyoming. The leases were worth millions of dollars, and the companies made personal "gifts" to Fall totaling more than $400,000. After a series of trials, Fall was convicted of receiving bribes and sentenced to prison. He was the first cabinet member ever imprisoned for a crime related to his official duties.

Even though Americans were shocked by the various wrongdoings, few blamed Calvin Coolidge. They noted that the new president was moving swiftly to "clean up the mess." When investigators found evidence that Attorney General Harry Daugherty was involved in questionable activities, Coolidge took action. He requested and received Daugherty's resignation. He appointed respected law school dean Harlan Stone as attorney general with instructions to weed out corruption in the Justice Department and restore confidence in the country's justice system. Coolidge later appointed Stone, a fellow graduate of Amherst, to the U.S. Supreme Court.

The public also got to know and admire the Coolidge family. Grace Coolidge rarely spoke publicly, but she appeared often at charitable and social events. Her photographs became familiar to readers of newspapers across the country. In those days, newspapers were just beginning to use human interest photographs. The two Coolidge sons were also in the news. John was away at school except in the summer. Calvin Jr., who was 15, lived with his parents in the White House.

"Keep Cool With Coolidge"

When the Republican Convention met in Cleveland in June 1924, there was no question the majority of the delegates wanted Coolidge to run for a full term as president. He won the nomination easily, and his campaign managers even dreamed up a snappy campaign slogan: "Keep Cool With Coolidge."

A major issue debated at the convention was who should be the vice presidential candidate. The convention finally nominated Charles G. Dawes, a successful business executive who had served as the first director of the Bureau of the Budget under President Harding. In addition, Dawes had just completed a report for the League of Nations, outlining steps to help Germany recover from a terrible

The Republican National Convention in Cleveland nominated Coolidge for president in June 1924. Coolidge did not attend, but listened to the proceedings by radio.

economic collapse. Dawes later received the 1925 Nobel Peace Prize for his masterly report. Dawes was a devoted Republican and an enthusiastic campaigner. He would be a big help to Coolidge and a plus on the Republican ticket.

A Simple Game of Tennis

Riding a wave a popularity that summer and looking forward to the fall campaign, Calvin Coolidge was brought suddenly to earth a few weeks after the convention by an event that seemed to make political victory unimportant.

Perhaps Calvin Jr. was the president's favorite person in all the world. His son was now 16 years old, a handsome and intelligent young man in everyone's opinion. Coolidge once said the boy's facial features reminded him of his own mother. In June 1924, Calvin Jr. played tennis with his brother on the White House lawn. He wore tennis shoes with no socks. The teenager developed a blister on one of his toes. He ignored the blister, probably hoping it would get better on its own. Instead it got worse. A doctor looked at Calvin's foot and feared a serious infection had set in. In those days, before the discovery of antibiotic drugs, infections could lead to blood poisoning, and blood poisoning could kill.

On July 3, Calvin's condition worsened and he was moved to Walter Reed Hospital in Washington. The president and the first lady visited the stricken boy often. Coolidge appeared frustrated that even though he was one of the most

The Coolidge family in a photo taken on June 30, 1924, after Calvin's nomination. Only seven days later, Calvin Jr. (left) died of an infection that originated in a blister on his foot.

powerful people on Earth, he was powerless to help his son. Coolidge wrote, "In his [Calvin's] suffering he was asking me to make him well. I could not."

Late in the evening of July 7, 1924, Calvin Coolidge Jr. died. Grief-stricken, President Coolidge was never the same man again. He spent long hours

The President and the Nameless Boy

People across the country sent messages of condolence to the Coolidge family, and some came to the White House to deliver their messages personally. Colonel Edmund Starling, Coolidge's bodyguard, wrote of one incident a few days after young Calvin's death.

Very early one morning when I came to the White House, I saw a small boy standing at the fence, his face pressed against the iron railings. I asked him what he was doing up so early. He looked up at me, his eyes large and round and said, "I thought I might see the president. I heard he gets up early and takes a walk. I wanted to tell him how sorry I am that his little boy died."

Starling took the boy to Coolidge, but the boy simply stood before the president, unable to say a word.

The youngster was overwhelmed with awe and could not deliver his message, so I did it for him. The president had a difficult time controlling his emotions. When the lad had gone and we were walking through Lafayette Park, he said to me: "Colonel, whenever a boy wants to see me, always bring him in. Never turn him away or make him wait."

☆ ☆ ☆

Calvin and Grace Coolidge visit the grave of Calvin Jr. The president grieved the loss of his son for the rest of his life.

gazing silently from his office window down at the tennis court where his son played that simple game of tennis. Coolidge admitted the despair he felt affected his job performance. He wrote, "When [Calvin Jr.] went, the power and the glory of the Presidency went with him."

Grace Coolidge composed a poem, called "The Open Door," to honor her son. It included these words:

> You, my son,
>
> Have shown me God.
>
> Your kiss upon my cheek
>
> Has made me feel the gentle touch
>
> Of Him who leads us on.

Chapter 5

Re-election

While the Coolidge family struggled with the illness and death of Calvin Jr., the Democrats met to nominate their candidate for president. In a tumultuous convention that lasted 17 days, they conducted 104 ballots before nominating compromise candidate John W. Davis. Davis was a West Virginian who served as Woodrow Wilson's ambassador to Great Britain during World War I and later became a prominent lawyer in New York City. Nebraska governor Charles W. Bryan was nominated for vice president.

A third party, the Progressive party, nominated Republican senator Robert LaFollette of Wisconsin. The Progressives appealed to dissatisfied Republican and Democratic voters who wanted a more active and reform-minded government. The country remained in a Republican mood, however. Coolidge beat the Democrat John Davis

Above, a 1924 Republican poster for Coolidge and Dawes. At right, a cartoon shows the 1924 candidates offering sweets to the "voter." Coolidge offers "common sense," Democratic candidate John Davis offers "equality," and Progressive candidate Robert LaFollette offers "reform." Coolidge won the election easily.

In 1925, for the first time ever, the president's inaugural address was broadcast on the radio. The oath of office was administered by Chief Justice Taft, who had served as president from 1909 to 1913. This was the first time an ex-president swore in another president.

Chief Justice William Howard Taft (left) administers the oath of office to President Coolidge (right) on March 4, 1925. Taft had served as president from 1909 to 1913.

by a margin of almost two votes to one, and LaFollette finished a distant third. The vote count proved the American people wanted to "Keep Cool with Coolidge."

Calvin Coolidge took his oath of office on the steps of the Capitol Building on March 4, 1925. Chief Justice of the United States William Howard Taft swore him in. This swearing-in was starkly different from the first time Coolidge took the oath, administered by his own father by the light of a kerosene lamp. Then he was an "accidental president," raised to high office by the death of Warren Harding. Now he was president on his own.

The Haves and the Have-Nots of the 1920s ——

Coolidge once said, "The man who builds a factory builds a temple. . . . The man who works there worships there." The words reflect his belief that American business—not government—was the source of national prosperity. In the mid-1920s, it seemed this belief was fully justified. American factories astonished the world with their production of new automobiles, radios, refrigerators, and

Car Culture

The automobile industry was one of the fastest growing and most prosperous industries in the country. By 1927 the United States had one car for every 5 people, compared to one for every 43 persons in Great Britain, and one for every 325 persons in Italy.

★★☆

other consumer goods. The middle class, including millions who worked in American factories, never had it so good.

Not all Americans shared in the prosperity, however. Many groups, including African Americans and the nation's farmers, were left behind. A large number of America's 10.5 million blacks lived in some degree of poverty. In the South many were landless sharecroppers who farmed land they did not own. Sharecroppers paid high rents to the landowners, and the payments kept them poor. Conditions were not much better in the North. African Americans who moved to the northern states in the 1920s discovered that most promising jobs were closed to them because employers hired only whites.

With discrimination common in both the North and South, there was no large movement to improve conditions for African Americans. Still, the president was eager to keep their traditional support for the Republican party. In a speech at the all-black Howard University, he pointed out the progress African Americans had made since the end of slavery 60 years earlier: "More than 80 percent of all American Negroes [then the polite term for African Americans] are now able to read and write; when they achieved their freedom not 10 percent were literate. There are nearly 2,000,000 Negro pupils in the public schools; well-nigh 40,000 Negro teachers are listed, more than 3000 following their profession in normal [teacher-training] schools and colleges."

Farmers suffered major setbacks during the otherwise prosperous 1920s. During World War I, prices for food crops shot upward and farmers thrived. After the war, prices dropped and never regained their wartime highs. At the same time, large farming enterprises were using new machinery to farm ever larger plots. Fewer workers were needed to plant and harvest crops. Small farmers, who could not afford the new farm implements, could not compete and were moving off the land into towns and cities. The farm population was diminishing.

Pressure grew in Congress to provide some relief for the farming community. In 1927 Congress passed the McNary-Haugen Farm Relief Bill which established a government organization to buy surplus crops from farmers at set prices and take responsibility for selling them at home or overseas. It was a bold plan, and farmers hoped the measure would help them survive by keeping prices up.

Others in the country were against the bill, fearing that it would increase prices for food. President Coolidge *vetoed* the bill (refused to sign it into law). He believed deeply that the marketplace, not the government, should determine the price of goods. Many farmers were bitter that Coolidge, who grew up a farmer, would oppose a law designed to help those who tilled the soil. When Congress passed the bill again in 1928, Coolidge vetoed it again. Both times, Congress was

President Coolidge with Secretary of Commerce Herbert Hoover, a leading member of the cabinet.

unable to *override* Coolidge's veto (pass it by two-thirds majorities to make it law), and the McNary-Haugen plan never went into effect.

Even though some were left out of the Coolidge Prosperity, the president's popularity remained high. Many Americans agreed with Coolidge that government should remain limited and that a free marketplace brought good times. For that reason, they didn't expect their political leaders to be heroes. The heroes of the Roaring Twenties were giants of sports and adventure: Babe Ruth, who hit a record 60 home runs in 1927, and Charles Lindbergh, who became the first to fly across the Atlantic alone the same year. The quiet man in the White House was expected to run the country in a proper manner. This he did while the great party that was the 1920s rolled on.

The World Abroad

Most Americans had approved when the United States entered World War I in 1917. After the war, however, they changed their minds. More than 50,000 Americans were killed, and the war cost the country billions of dollars. Yet it seemed America gained little for its efforts. As a result, American voters came to favor *isolationism*, a policy that limited the involvement of the United States in world affairs. Isolationists pointed out that the nation was protected from possible

Banner headlines announce that Charles Lindbergh has become the first person to fly solo across the Atlantic Ocean. Coolidge later invited Lindbergh to the White House.

enemies by two large oceans, and favored steering clear of international conflicts, especially in Europe.

For the most part, President Coolidge agreed with isolationist thinking, but as president he still had to carry on diplomatic relations with other countries. In one respect, he challenged isolationism, urging that the United States join the World Court. The court, established by the League of Nations, provided a forum for settling legal disputes between countries. Coolidge's profound respect for law led him to believe an international court would promote peace. Isolationist thinking was too strong, however. The Senate, responding to the mood of voters, blocked Coolidge's efforts to join the World Court.

The president had greater success with the Kellogg-Briand Pact. The agreement, negotiated by his secretary of state, Frank Kellogg, and French foreign minister Aristide Briand, was a high-minded statement in which countries renounced war as a way to settle their disputes. By 1928, 15 nations, including the United States, signed the Kellogg-Briand Pact. Since the agreement provided no way to enforce peace, it proved to be of little use. When wars began to break out in the 1930s, the signers of the pact were helpless to end them.

The most serious international issue during Coolidge's term was repayment of war loans. During World War I, the United States loaned its allies, primarily Britain and France, some $10 billion. Wartime agreements said the loans

President Calvin Coolidge.

were to be paid back at 5 percent interest. After the war, the debtor nations were unable to make their payments, and the amounts they owed were increasing. Many advisers urged the president to forgive the debts. Coolidge disagreed. According to one story, he said, "They hired [borrowed] the money, didn't they?" In the end, Coolidge agreed to ease the debt burdens by allowing more time for debtor nations to pay.

There was no way the United States could isolate itself from Mexico, its neighbor to the south. During the 1920s, Mexico's revolutionary government began taking over U.S.-owned companies within its borders, creating anger in the United States. In 1927 Coolidge appointed Dwight Morrow, a prominent New York lawyer and an old friend, as ambassador to Mexico. Coolidge trusted Morrow and gave him a free hand to improve U.S. relations with the Mexican government. Morrow was so successful that he remained at his post even after

Ten Troubles

Some political leaders warned Coolidge that Communists were behind Mexico's takeover of U.S. businesses. They urged him to send troops into the country. Coolidge urged patience. He once said, "If you see ten troubles coming down the road, you can be sure that nine of them will run into a ditch before they reach you."

☆☆☆

Coolidge left the presidency. Morrow's daughter Anne married the celebrated pilot Charles Lindbergh. Later, as Anne Morrow Lindbergh, she became a much admired author.

Life in the White House ——————————

Calvin Coolidge brought his farm work habits to the presidency. Typically he rose at six in the morning. He had breakfast, reading newspapers as he ate. He worked from nine to twelve and broke for a light lunch. Often he took a nap after lunch, another habit he acquired from the farm. He worked again until six, ate dinner, and was in bed by ten. His early-to-bed early-to-rise work habits were reported in the newspapers. One night he broke his usual pattern and went to see a popular stage comedy called *Animal Crackers*. Near the end of the performance, the leading comic, Groucho Marx, looked out into the audience and pointed to the president. "Isn't it past your bedtime, Calvin?" he asked.

The president often had a sense of humor about himself. He allowed himself to be photographed in outlandish attire including cowboy outfits and Indian warbonnets. In the White House, he exercised on an electrically operated mechanical horse. He whooped like a cowboy when he rode the contraption. When an aide warned that people might laugh if they saw him on the artificial horse, he said, "Well, it's good for people to laugh."

The Marx Brothers, leading comedy stars of the day. Groucho (center) teased Coolidge about his early bedtime during a performance in Washington.

Coolidge was also fond of playing practical jokes. On his desk were half a dozen buzzers, each of which summoned a different assistant. Sometimes he pressed all the buzzers simultaneously to see who would come running into his office first.

Both Calvin and Grace Coolidge loved animals. Their favorite pet was a white collie named Rob Roy. At formal dinner parties the president often seemed more interested in feeding scraps to Rob Roy than in making conversation with his guests. The family owned a cat called Tige that had a habit of jumping on the president's shoulder and draping herself around his neck. The pet that only the Coolidges liked was a raccoon named Rebecca. Over the objections of the staff, Rebecca was given the run of the White House.

Grace Coolidge was the social center of the White House. Many observers claimed she was the most attractive first lady in the country's history. She hosted many parties at the mansion. The president came to these affairs only with great reluctance. Grace Coolidge dressed in fine style. Calvin still controlled the family budget, and he was known to be a skinflint, but he encouraged his wife to choose her clothes from the most expensive shops.

In March 1926, sorrow once more entered the Coolidge family's life. The president's 80-year-old father became gravely ill. Calvin longed to be at his father's side, but work kept him in the White House. Finally, when his father's condition worsened, the president took a special train to Vermont. However, John Coolidge died before his son arrived. Coolidge wrote, "When I reached home he was gone. It cost a great deal to be President."

In the summer of 1927, the Coolidges broke their usual reluctance to travel and vacationed in the Black Hills of South Dakota. On the morning of August 2, the president summoned reporters to the lodge where he and Mrs. Coolidge were staying. He handed them each a statement, which read, "I do not choose to run for president in nineteen twenty-eight."

Once again, Calvin Coolidge wasted no words and provided no explanation. People were shocked and amused. He even took his wife by surprise. He would easily be elected if he decided to run. Around the country people asked, Why? Coolidge probably believed a change in leadership would be good for the country. As he wrote, "The chances of having wise and faithful public service are increased by a change in the presidential office after a moderate length of time."

In the summer of 1928, the Republican National Convention nominated Herbert Hoover to run for president. Hoover had served as secretary of commerce under presidents Harding and Coolidge, and had gained widespread admiration for organizing relief efforts in Europe during World War I. In 1927 he had

On inauguration day in 1929, Coolidge (left) rides to the ceremony with incoming president Herbert Hoover.

directed a large relief program at home to help thousands made homeless by a great flood on the lower Mississippi River. In November Hoover was elected, becoming the third Republican president in a row.

On March 3, 1929, Calvin Coolidge left the White House. As he boarded the train for his home in Massachusetts, he waved to reporters. "Good-bye," he said. "I have had a very enjoyable time in Washington."

Chapter 6

The Ex-President

In retirement, Calvin and Grace Coolidge returned to Northampton, where they first met. Coolidge turned to writing. He wrote *The Autobiography of Calvin Coolidge* as well as articles for leading magazines. One of his major writing projects was a series of newspaper columns called "Thinking Things Over With Calvin Coolidge." His writings earned a good deal of money. The family soon moved to a larger house, part of a 9-acre (3.6-hectare) estate called The Beeches.

Coolidge worked as a trustee for his beloved Amherst College. He entertained old friends including Frank Stearns. Sometimes he attended meetings of the Northampton Literary Club to hear discussions on the latest books. Often he simply sat on his porch and felt the afternoon breezes.

Coolidge fishing at a lake in Connecticut during his retirement. He died in 1933.

Depression

In October 1929, seven months after Coolidge left the White House, the stock market in New York crashed. As the value of stocks plunged, hundreds of investors were ruined, and confidence in the nation's economy was shaken. The crash proved to be the beginning of the longest and most difficult economic depression in the nation's history. Banks failed, millions lost their jobs, and many were hungry and homeless. People pleaded with President Hoover to take action to ease the suffering. Hoover and Congress began limited programs designed to put businesses back on their feet, but nothing seemed to help. Soon Hoover was receiving much of the blame for the deepening depression. Shantytowns built by the homeless were called Hoovervilles.

The depression continued through Hoover's term. In 1932 Republicans nominated him for re-election, but Democratic candidate Franklin D. Roosevelt was elected by a landslide. This ended the Republicans' twelve-year hold on the presidency. Looking back, voters wondered if the policies of Harding, Coolidge, and Hoover had helped bring on the Great Depression.

Last Days

On the morning of January 5, 1933, Coolidge rose early. He had not been feeling well. At a New Year's party days earlier, he told friends, "I'm afraid I'm all

After Coolidge's death, Grace Coolidge moved to a smaller house in Northampton, where she lived until her death at age 78, on July 8, 1957. Calvin Coolidge once said of his wife, "For almost a quarter of a century she has borne with my infirmities, and I have rejoiced in her graces."

★ ★ ☆

burned out." Late that morning he sat in his study and fitted in a few pieces of a jigsaw puzzle bearing the face of George Washington. A handyman came to the house to repair the furnace, and Coolidge said cheerfully, "Good morning, Robert." Those were his last words. Coolidge went upstairs to his bedroom, where he collapsed and died of a heart attack. He was 60 years old.

The funeral for Calvin Coolidge took place in the Congregational Church in Northampton, where he and Grace had long been faithful members. He was buried in the Plymouth Notch cemetery in Plymouth, Vermont, near his parents and his sister.

Historians Look at the Coolidge Presidency —

In 1962 the distinguished historian Arthur M. Schlesinger surveyed 75 historians, asking them to rank all the presidents into five categories: great, near great, average, below average, and failures. In the poll, Coolidge was placed in the "below average" category, ranking 27th of the 31 presidents included. The historians criticized Coolidge not so much for what he did, but for what he failed to do. They cited his failure to use his influence to end trading abuses in the stock market and his reluctance to involve the United States in world affairs. In another poll of historians published in 1982, Coolidge ranked 27th of 38 presidents.

Many historians today are less critical of Calvin Coolidge. Conservative Republican policies gained popularity once again in the 1980s, and conservative leaders raised many of the same questions Coolidge had raised. Like him, they favored smaller, less intrusive government and less regulation of business. They suggested that Coolidge's view of government was sound. Even his supporters concede that Coolidge was no miracle-worker. As president he was more a manager than a leader. He was also not a prophet and could not know that economic depression and war would follow his presidency.

Finally, students of Coolidge's life and times agree that he had virtues not shared by many other presidents. They point especially to his deep belief that holding high office is a form of public service, not a way of satisfying personal ambitions for greatness or riches. As historian Robert H. Ferrell wrote in his study of Coolidge, "Last among Coolidge's traits, and it overshadowed the others in determining the course of his presidency, was his sense of public service. . . . Coolidge's critics could not understand this part of the president's makeup."

Calvin Coolidge would have agreed. Shortly after he became president, Coolidge wrote to his friend Frank Stearns, "I am going to try to do what seems best for the country, and get what satisfaction I can out of that. Most everything else will take care of itself."

Fast Facts   Calvin Coolidge

Birth:	July 4, 1872
Birthplace:	Plymouth, Vermont
Parents:	John Calvin Coolidge and Victoria Moor Coolidge
Sister:	Abigail Gratia Coolidge (1875–1890)
Education:	Amherst College, Amherst, Massachusetts; graduated 1895
Occupation:	Lawyer and politician
Marriage:	To Grace Anna Goodhue on October 4, 1905
Children:	(see First Lady Fast Facts at right)
Political Party:	Republican
Public Offices:	1899 City Councilman, Northampton, Massachusetts
	1900–1901 City Solicitor, Northampton
	1903 Clerk of the Hampshire County Court
	1907–1908 Massachusetts House of Representatives
	1910–1911 Mayor of Northampton
	1912–1915 Massachusetts Senate
	1916–1918 Lieutenant Governor of Massachusetts
	1919 Governor of Massachusetts
	1921–1923 Vice President of the United States
	1923–1929 30th President of the United States
His Vice President:	1925–1929 Charles G. Dawes (1865-1951)
Major Actions as President:	1924 Signed a revised immigration law
	1925 Sent U.S. Marines to Nicaragua
	1927 Vetoed the McNary-Haugen farm bill
	1927 Favored the Kellogg-Briand Pact
Death:	January 5, 1933
Age at Death:	60 years
Burial Place:	Plymouth Notch Cemetery, Plymouth, Vermont

Fast Facts Grace Anna Coolidge

Birth:	January 3, 1879
Birthplace:	Burlington, Vermont
Parents:	Andrew Goodhue and Lemira Barrett Goodhue
Brothers & Sisters:	None
Education:	University of Vermont, graduated 1902
Marriage:	To Calvin Coolidge, October 4, 1905
Children:	John Coolidge (1906–2000)
	Calvin Coolidge Jr. (1908–1924)
Death:	July 8, 1957
Age at Death:	78 years
Burial Place:	Plymouth Notch Cemetery, Plymouth, Vermont

Timeline

1872	1879	1884	1890	1891
Calvin Coolidge born July 4, in Plymouth Notch, Vermont	Coolidge's future wife, Grace Goodhue, born in Burlington, Vermont	Coolidge's mother dies	Sister Abigail dies at age 15	Coolidge enrolls at Amherst College, Amherst, Massachusetts

1906	1908	1909	1911	1914
Son John is born; Coolidge elected to Massachusetts House of Representatives, serves two terms	Son Calvin Jr. is born	Coolidge elected mayor of Northampton	Elected to Massachusetts State Senate, serves 1912–1915	World War I begins in Europe

1921	1923	1924	1925	1926
Sworn in as vice president	President Harding dies August 2, Coolidge sworn in as president August 3	Son Calvin Jr. dies of blood poisoning, July; Coolidge elected to full term as president, November	Inaugurated in Washington, D.C.	Coolidge's father dies in Plymouth Notch, Vermont

1895	1897	1899	1900	1905
Graduates from Amherst; moves to Northampton, Massachusetts, to study law	Licensed to practice law, begins practice in Northampton	Serves as city councilman, Northampton, Massachusetts	Becomes Northampton city solicitor	Calvin Coolidge and Grace Goodhue marry

1915	1917	1918	1919	1920
Coolidge elected state lieutenant governor, serves 1916–1918	The United States enters World War I	Coolidge elected governor of Massachusetts; World War I ends	Gains national fame for his firm actions in the Boston Police Strike	Gains Republican nomination for vice president, June; elected, November

1927	1929	1932	1933
Charles Lindbergh makes the first solo flight across the Atlantic Ocean; Coolidge announces he will not run for a second full term	Herbert Hoover inaugurated president, March; stock market crash begins the Great Depression, October	Franklin D. Roosevelt elected president	Calvin Coolidge dies January 5, at age 60

The New York Times.

LINDBERGH DOES IT! TO PARIS IN 33½ HOURS;
FLIES 1,000 MILES THROUGH SNOW AND SLEET;
CHEERING FRENCH CARRY HIM OFF FIELD

Glossary

armistice: an agreement to end fighting while a peace agreement is negotiated

bootlegger: a person who manufactures and transports illegal alcoholic beverages

city solicitor: a lawyer who represents a city in legal disputes

favorite son: a person nominated at a political convention by his state's delegation as a sign of respect

isolationism: in U.S. politics, the belief that the United States should avoid an active role in world affairs

override: in U.S. government, the passage of a bill into law by two-thirds majorities in the legislature after the president (or state governor) has vetoed the bill; *see* veto

prophetic: able to predict future events

radical: a political belief considered extreme or dangerous by the community

ratify: to approve a law or action officially; according to the U.S. Constitution, the U.S. Senate must ratify treaties with foreign governments

stoical: unaffected by good or ill fortune

stroke: stoppage of blood circulation in the brain, often leading to paralysis or other disabilities

veto: in U.S. government, the refusal of a president (or state governor) to sign into law a bill passed by the Congress (or legislature)

women's suffrage: the campaign to gain women the right to vote

Further Reading

Allen, Michael Geoffrey. *Calvin Coolidge*. Berkeley Heights, NJ: Enslow Publishers, 2002.

Dolan, Edward. *America in World War I*. Brookfield, CT: Millbrook Press, 1996.

Fisher, Leonard Everett. *The White House*. New York: Holiday House, 1989.

Majure, Janet. *Elections*. San Diego, CA: Lucent Books, 1996.

Stein, R. Conrad. *The Roaring Twenties*. Danbury, CT: Children's Press, 1994.

Wade, Linda R. *Warren G. Harding: Twenty-ninth President of the United States*. Danbury CT: Children's Press, 1989.

MORE ADVANCED READING

Coolidge, Calvin. *The Autobiography of Calvin Coolidge*. Plymouth, VT: Calvin Coolidge Memorial Foundation, 1989.

Ferrell, Robert H. *The Presidency of Calvin Coolidge*. Lawrence: University of Kansas Press, 1998.

Sobel, Robert. *Coolidge: An American Enigma*. Washington, DC: Regnery Publishers, 1998.

★ ★ ★ ★

Calvin Coolidge Homestead Historic Site
P.O. Box 97
Plymouth Notch, VT 05056
(802) 672-3389

This site includes the Coolidge farm and home, the one-room schoolhouse he attended, and other attractions. The settings are largely unchanged since 1923, when Coolidge became president.

Calvin Coolidge Presidential Library and Museum
20 West Street
Northampton, MA 01060
(413) 587-1011

The museum displays manuscripts, letters, and personal and presidential papers of the president and first lady. Also in Northampton is the house at 21 Massasoit Street, where the Coolidge family lived for more than 20 years and The Beeches, where they lived in retirement.

Online Sites of Interest

★ **The White House**

http://www.whitehouse.gov/history/presidents/cc30.html

A brief biography of Calvin Coolidge. The White House site also offers additional information on the executive mansion and the present administration.

★ **Calvin Coolidge Memorial Foundation**

http://www.calvin-coolidge.org/

Provides a valuable chronology of Coolidge's life and career, and links to many useful online resources.

★ **American President**

http://www.americanpresident.org/history/calvincoolidge/

Provides a useful biography of Coolidge with a timeline and additional information on his wife, cabinet members, and staff. The site is managed by the University of Virginia and offers comparable material on all of the presidents.

★ **Grolier: The American Presidency**

http://ap.grolier.com/

Provides several biographies of each president at different reading levels.

Table of Presidents

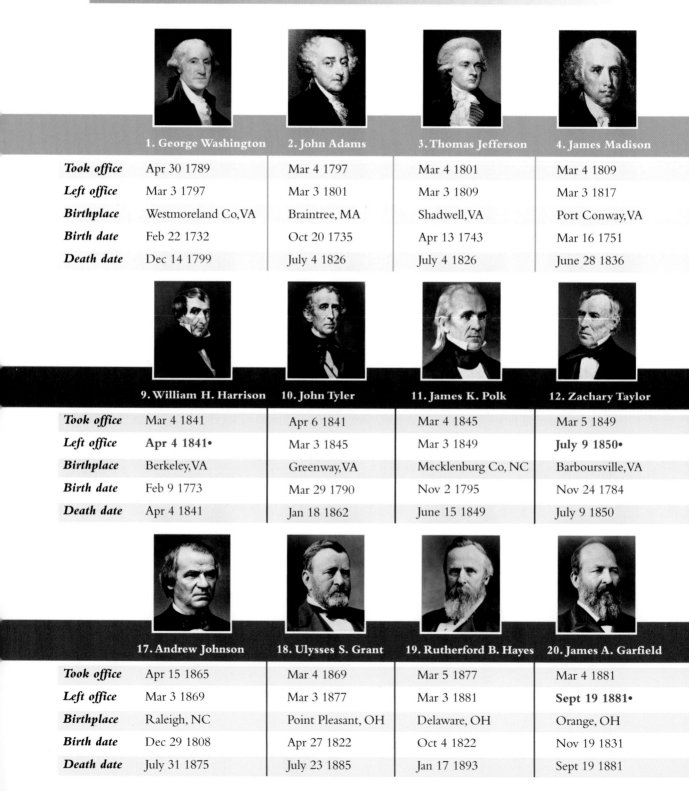

	1. George Washington	2. John Adams	3. Thomas Jefferson	4. James Madison
Took office	Apr 30 1789	Mar 4 1797	Mar 4 1801	Mar 4 1809
Left office	Mar 3 1797	Mar 3 1801	Mar 3 1809	Mar 3 1817
Birthplace	Westmoreland Co, VA	Braintree, MA	Shadwell, VA	Port Conway, VA
Birth date	Feb 22 1732	Oct 20 1735	Apr 13 1743	Mar 16 1751
Death date	Dec 14 1799	July 4 1826	July 4 1826	June 28 1836

	9. William H. Harrison	10. John Tyler	11. James K. Polk	12. Zachary Taylor
Took office	Mar 4 1841	Apr 6 1841	Mar 4 1845	Mar 5 1849
Left office	Apr 4 1841•	Mar 3 1845	Mar 3 1849	July 9 1850•
Birthplace	Berkeley, VA	Greenway, VA	Mecklenburg Co, NC	Barboursville, VA
Birth date	Feb 9 1773	Mar 29 1790	Nov 2 1795	Nov 24 1784
Death date	Apr 4 1841	Jan 18 1862	June 15 1849	July 9 1850

	17. Andrew Johnson	18. Ulysses S. Grant	19. Rutherford B. Hayes	20. James A. Garfield
Took office	Apr 15 1865	Mar 4 1869	Mar 5 1877	Mar 4 1881
Left office	Mar 3 1869	Mar 3 1877	Mar 3 1881	Sept 19 1881•
Birthplace	Raleigh, NC	Point Pleasant, OH	Delaware, OH	Orange, OH
Birth date	Dec 29 1808	Apr 27 1822	Oct 4 1822	Nov 19 1831
Death date	July 31 1875	July 23 1885	Jan 17 1893	Sept 19 1881

5. James Monroe	6. John Quincy Adams	7. Andrew Jackson	8. Martin Van Buren
Mar 4 1817	Mar 4 1825	Mar 4 1829	Mar 4 1837
Mar 3 1825	Mar 3 1829	Mar 3 1837	Mar 3 1841
Westmoreland Co, VA	Braintree, MA	The Waxhaws, SC	Kinderhook, NY
Apr 28 1758	July 11 1767	Mar 15 1767	Dec 5 1782
July 4 1831	Feb 23 1848	June 8 1845	July 24 1862

13. Millard Fillmore	14. Franklin Pierce	15. James Buchanan	16. Abraham Lincoln
July 9 1850	Mar 4 1853	Mar 4 1857	Mar 4 1861
Mar 3 1853	Mar 3 1857	Mar 3 1861	**Apr 15 1865•**
Locke Township, NY	Hillsborough, NH	Cove Gap, PA	Hardin Co, KY
Jan 7 1800	Nov 23 1804	Apr 23 1791	Feb 12 1809
Mar 8 1874	Oct 8 1869	June 1 1868	Apr 15 1865

21. Chester A. Arthur	22. Grover Cleveland	23. Benjamin Harrison	24. Grover Cleveland
Sept 19 1881	Mar 4 1885	Mar 4 1889	Mar 4 1893
Mar 3 1885	Mar 3 1889	Mar 3 1893	Mar 3 1897
Fairfield, VT	Caldwell, NJ	North Bend, OH	Caldwell, NJ
Oct 5 1829	Mar 18 1837	Aug 20 1833	Mar 18 1837
Nov 18 1886	June 24 1908	Mar 13 1901	June 24 1908

	25. William McKinley	26. Theodore Roosevelt	27. William H. Taft	28. Woodrow Wilson
Took office	Mar 4 1897	Sept 14 1901	Mar 4 1909	Mar 4 1913
Left office	Sept 14 1901•	Mar 3 1909	Mar 3 1913	Mar 3 1921
Birthplace	Niles, OH	New York, NY	Cincinnati, OH	Staunton, VA
Birth date	Jan 29 1843	Oct 27 1858	Sept 15 1857	Dec 28 1856
Death date	Sept 14 1901	Jan 6 1919	Mar 8 1930	Feb 3 1924

	33. Harry S. Truman	34. Dwight D. Eisenhower	35. John F. Kennedy	36. Lyndon B. Johnson
Took office	Apr 12 1945	Jan 20 1953	Jan 20 1961	Nov 22 1963
Left office	Jan 20 1953	Jan 20 1961	Nov 22 1963•	Jan 20 1969
Birthplace	Lamar, MO	Denison, TX	Brookline, MA	Johnson City, TX
Birth date	May 8 1884	Oct 14 1890	May 29 1917	Aug 27 1908
Death date	Dec 26 1972	Mar 28 1969	Nov 22 1963	Jan 22 1973

	41. George Bush	42. Bill Clinton	43. George W. Bush	
Took office	Jan 20 1989	Jan 20 1993	Jan 20 2001	
Left office	Jan 20 1993	Jan 20 2001	—	
Birthplace	Milton, MA	Hope, AR	New Haven, CT	
Birth date	June 12 1924	Aug 19 1946	July 6 1946	
Death date	—	—	—	

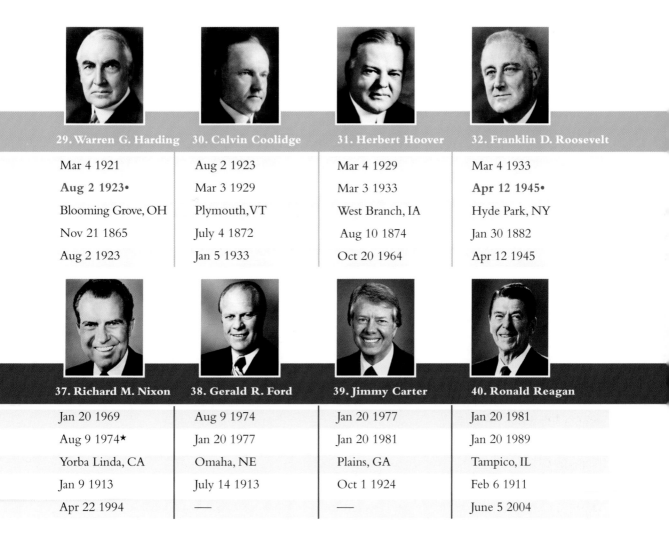

29. Warren G. Harding	30. Calvin Coolidge	31. Herbert Hoover	32. Franklin D. Roosevelt
Mar 4 1921	Aug 2 1923	Mar 4 1929	Mar 4 1933
Aug 2 1923•	Mar 3 1929	Mar 3 1933	**Apr 12 1945•**
Blooming Grove, OH	Plymouth, VT	West Branch, IA	Hyde Park, NY
Nov 21 1865	July 4 1872	Aug 10 1874	Jan 30 1882
Aug 2 1923	Jan 5 1933	Oct 20 1964	Apr 12 1945

37. Richard M. Nixon	38. Gerald R. Ford	39. Jimmy Carter	40. Ronald Reagan
Jan 20 1969	Aug 9 1974	Jan 20 1977	Jan 20 1981
Aug 9 1974★	Jan 20 1977	Jan 20 1981	Jan 20 1989
Yorba Linda, CA	Omaha, NE	Plains, GA	Tampico, IL
Jan 9 1913	July 14 1913	Oct 1 1924	Feb 6 1911
Apr 22 1994	—	—	June 5 2004

• Indicates the president died while in office.

★ Richard Nixon resigned before his term expired.

Index

★ ★ ★ ★

Page numbers in *italics* indicate illustrations.

About the Author

R. Conrad Stein was born and raised in Chicago. At age 18 he enlisted in the U.S. Marines and served three years. He later attended the University of Illinois and graduated with a degree in history. Mr. Stein is a full-time writer of books for young readers, and over the years he has published more than 100 titles. Most of his published works have been history and geography books. The author lives in Chicago with his wife, children's book author Deborah Kent, and their daughter Janna.